W9-AAE-629

Presented to

my favorite Beverly .... forever

by

Anna

Thank you for your
Friendship ~
you're dear ....

9/01

The
CHARM
of
SIMPLE
THINGS

COUNTRYMAN™

Copyright of text © 1998 by J. Countryman
Copyright of illustrations © 1998 by Maren Scott
Copyright of photos ©1998 by Tracey Elliot-Reep

Published by J. Countryman, a division of Thomas Nelson Inc., Nashville, Tennessee 37214

Compiled and edited by Terri Gibbs

All rights reserved.

No portion of this publication may be reproduced, stored in a retrieval system or transmitted in any form by any means—electronic, mechanical, photo-copying, recording, or any other—except for brief quotations in printed reviews, without the prior written permission of the publisher.

A J. Countryman Book
J. Countryman is a registered trademark

Designed by Left Coast Design
Portland, Oregon

ISBN: 0-8499-1503-1

Made in Belgium

Introduction

What are the simple things that make life so enjoyable?

    a picnic basket of fried chicken and corn fritters

    hot chocolate beside a crackling fire

    warm peach pie with fresh whipped cream

    wild roses growing in profusion over a garden trellis

    jars of summer bounty crowding grandmother's pantry shelves

Just thinking of them brings a smile—a longing for life to move at a more leisurely pace.

And there are simple things of the heart. Music, laughter, acts of kindness, family, friends, good manners, and serendipitous surprises. These are the simple pleasures we enjoy, the pleasures we love to give and receive.

Around the corner of the next page, we invite you to ramble down the lanes of simple times, to poke merrily through nooks and crannies filled with simple things. And we are sure that as Laura Ingalls Wilder once said, "You will be surprised how much of an adventure can enter into ordinary things."

Terri Gibbs
Editor

Delight in Simple Things

Learn to like what does not cost much.

Learn to like reading, conversation, music.

Learn to like plain food, plain service, plain cooking.

Learn to like people, even those who may be very different from you.

Learn to shelter your family with love, comfort, and peace.

Learn to keep your wants simple. Refuse to be owned and anchored by things and opinions of others.

Learn to like the sunrise and the sunset, the beating of rain on the roof and windows, the gentle fall of snow in winter.

Learn to hold heaven near and dear.

Learn to love God, for He surely loves you.

Anonymous

LEARN TO LIKE WHAT DOES NOT COST MUCH.

LEARN TO LIKE READING, CONVERSATION, MUSIC.

We gather simple pleasures like daisies by the way.

Louisa May Alcott

*M*ost of us, if we are honest with ourselves, will admit that we live too fast, too erratically, too crudely, and too thoughtlessly. The remedy or antidote for all of this is to live gently.

W. Phillip Keller
Taming Tension

It's the Bits and Pieces that Count

Women would like to make one big spiritual sacrifice. We would like to do one grand thing and be assured everything will work out well. But we can't. It's the bits and pieces put together year after year that count. Sometimes we don't see meaning in the little things and we are not conscious of how it all works together to create a powerful image.

The little things we do at home, like putting wildflowers in a vase, are invisible medicine for all the bumps and bruises of family life. The connections we make in our daily rounds, an old photograph tucked into a frame, a lullaby each evening by the bedside, a hug among fresh clean linens, are the putty that holds the mosaic together.

Ingrid Trobish
Keeper of the Springs

The Beauty of Everyday Life

The true way to live is to enjoy every moment as it passes, and surely it is in the everyday things around us that the beauty of life lies. . . .

I have never lost my childhood delight in going after the cows. I still slip from other things for the sake of the walk through the pastures, down along the creek and over the hill to the farthest corner where the cows are usually found. Many a time, instead of me finding the cows, they, on their journey home, unurged, found me and took me home with them.

Laura Ingalls Wilder
Words from a Fearless Heart

A Simple Room

My living room is a simple, welcoming room. It's simplicity suits me—there I can relax and enjoy the sunlight. As in many homes, my living room is the first room guests see upon entering the house and that's important because it is a reflection of how I live. It is a place that soothes anxious feelings. . . .

Simplicity is not just another interior design option. It is also one of the great expressions of Christian faith. Simplicity is devoting our lives to one thing and one thing only—to loving the Lord our God with our whole being and our neighbors as ourselves.

Harriet Crosby
A Place Called Home

It is not how much we have,

but how much we enjoy it

that makes for happiness.

Anonymous

Two Small Rooms
in Switzerland

Our total [living] space consists of these two small bedrooms. . . . The price is cheaper than other pensions, and the house is scrupulously clean. Mme. Turrian is very kind and pleasant and the view is a gift of the Lord. The trolley line ends two houses away, so transportation is close. We are in the highest part of Lausanne, just outside of the city limits. We have country sounds and smells all around us, the smell of hay and pine trees, and the constant music of tinkling cowbells. Priscilla, Susan, and Debby have very little indoor space, but the front garden goes downhill to a wall and has some lovely spots under the trees to play. The backyard goes straight up, and has a rabbit and chicken house in it. Priscilla is allowed to gather the two or three eggs that appear each day. The Lord is filling our needs in one way if not another!

Edith Schaeffer
The Tapestry

A letter is a simple thing...

In letters you explore the landscape of your soul and reveal it to a friend. . . . Sometimes the letter received from a friend wraps the soul in a warm blanket. Even the envelope is lovingly addressed by hand, the stamp carefully chosen and placed. It's easy to sift such letters from the daily avalanche of mail and patiently wait for the first uninterrupted moment to open such a treasure. Reading it is like opening a window with a striking view. What a luxury to think a thought to the end with pen and paper!

Katrine Stewart
in *Keeper of the Springs*

Instead of writing a letter from your computer keyboard, why not use a handsome pen and cream-colored paper to send a warm, friendly message written by hand. It is a personal reflection of your thoughts. Or take time to send

a note to _____

a card to _____

a post card to _____

a box of homemade goodies to _____

The success of our living is measured not by what we can accumulate for ourselves, but what we can bestow upon our fellow travelers on life's tough trail.

W. Phillip Keller

Our Small Thatched Hut

A fter marriage, Walter and I started off in a thatched-roof hut close to a dusty African village. Our days were full, taking care of practical, spiritual, and sometimes medical needs of villagers. Our lives were geared around basic necessities. But we did have a nice picture to look at and a china cup and saucer for tea. It was the meaning we gave to things we did have that enriched our sense of place.

We made sure we had good books in different languages and some kind of music. We had a little wind-up phonograph with three records we'd rotate and a small pump organ. . . . And always we had the stars. Each evening at dusk we would sit outside and watch them twinkle, fall, or move across the sky.

Ingrid Trobisch
Keeper of the Springs

Dear friend,

Beauty lies in
quiet things
And they are everywhere,
But we may fail to find them
Unless we pause for prayer.

June Masters Bacher
Quiet Moments for Women

I have come to realize, that the radiance of the rose and the whiteness of the lily do not take away the fragrance of the little violet or the delightful simplicity of the daisy. Perfection consists in being what God wants us to be.

Thérèse

A flower is a simple thing...

On early summer mornings when tiny, glistening drops of water clung to her flowers and garden plants, Old Missus Upjohn would be up and about. She would take a handmade basket with her, one that was flat. Then carefully she would gather dewy rose petals and take them directly to the springhouse, hoping they would last long enough for a neighbor or friend to stop by and share their beauty.

Jane Watson Hopping
The Lazy Days of Summer Cookbook

Lavender Potpourri

2 cups lavender flowers
1 cup white rose petals
1 cup red rose petals
5 drops lavender essential oil

Combine ingredients. Allow to set up in a closed container for 5-6 weeks, then put in sachet bags or an open bowl.

T. G.

One of the pleasures of summer is growing (or buying fresh) flowers that can be dried for winter bouquets. At our house we pick the flowers and hang them in small clusters on the clothesline in the shade. Some women hang flowers under the eaves of the house, where a light breeze dries them and the sun does not fade them.

Laura C. Martin
Handmade Gifts from a Country Garden

The symbolic messages of herbs and flowers:

angelica	*inspiration*	**burnet**	*a merry heart*
carnation	*bonds of affection*	**daisy**	*gentleness*
heartsease	*happy thoughts*	**ivy**	*friendship and fidelity*
lavender	*devotion*	**marjoram**	*joy and happiness*
mugwort	*happiness*	**myrtle**	*love and passion*
pansy	*"I think of you"*	**parsley**	*festivity*
rose	*love and desire*	**rosemary**	*remembrance*
sage	*wisdom*	**thyme**	*courage*

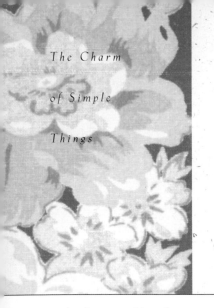

As I grow older the

simple pleasures of life

become even more

important.

Colette Bitker

A High Four-Poster Bed

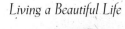

M y first memory of visiting my godmother in Framingham, Massachusetts, when I was five, was sleeping in the guest room in a high mahogany four-poster bed that faced a beautifully carved mantel; there was a crackling fire in the fireplace. I felt so utterly grown up! Next to the hearth was a shiny brass bucket full of pinecones that had been dipped in wax; the cones released reds, greens, and blues into the flames. I can still remember the crackle and the woody, smoky smells, and the heavenly feel of cool sheets and the creak of the bed as I looked across at the grown-up fire in my bedroom.

Alexandra Stoddard
Living a Beautiful Life

Timeless Treasures

There is a comfort in time-worn objects, a beauty in imperfection. Timeless treasures soothe our minds and bodies . . . and they don't cost much!

What timeless treasures would you add to the list?

antique family photos

church bells in the distance

pipe organ music

a toasty fire on a cold winter night

a hug from mom or dad

a comfy slip-covered armchair in the glow of an old floor lamp

_____

_____

_____

_____

_____

_____

_____

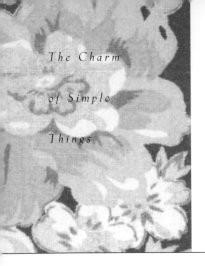

A Family Outing

When we forget the obvious, the little joys, the meals together, the birthday celebrations, the weeping together in time of pain, the wonder of the sunset or the daffodil peeping through the snow, we become less human.

Madeleine L'Engle

W hen the children were small, we would pack our gear and head for the hills to spend a night or a weekend. Once we made camp we would hike through the woods and sometimes walk as far as a nearby lake. In the evening we would cook chili, our favorite iron-kettle supper, over a campfire. Great dishesful served with warmed bread and cold milk settled us down for the night.

Wrapped in blankets, looking up at the stars, Raymond and I often thought that the woods must have been God's first cathedral. The silence, the softness of night-bird calls, and the whispering in the fir trees, left us full of tender emotions, a thankfulness for our two lovely children, for each other, for the beauty around us, and for all living creatures.

Jane Watson Hopping
The Lazy Days of Summer Cookbook

A book is a simple thing...

I love everything that's old; old friends, old times,
old manners, old books, old wines.

Oliver Goldsmith

A truly great book should be read in youth, again
in maturity, and once more in old age.

Robertson Davies

Favorite Books and Authors

_____

_____

_____

Books to Read

_____

_____

_____

Books to Buy

_____

_____

_____

If you are too busy to

read, you are too busy.

Richard J. Foster

A song is a simple thing...

I can't remember when I didn't sing, can't remember when the sight of a songbook or the sound of the radio or simply good spirits didn't set me going. In church or in the car, alone or with a chorus, I sing when I'm sad, sing when I'm happy, sing for no reason at all. If there's a simple source of joy in the world, it's this—lifting one's voice in music good, bad, or indifferent.

Church music was engraved on me at an early age, in a denomination known for its choirs. The words that were spoken were plain, unadorned, but when the choir got up to sing, and the congregation joined in, you could, as the hymns promised, feel a step away from Heaven. But then, these were my cradle songs, too. When we went to visit my Kentucky grandparents, we children were tucked in upstairs after dinner, while down below our aunts and uncles gathered round the piano, brought out the violin and trumpet and the hymn book. Chords, played with fervor, shook the floorboards as they worked their way through "The Old Rugged Cross" and on to "Abide With Me," and I sank into sleep dreaming of a God who looked a lot like my fiddle-playing grandfather.

Catherine Calvert
Victoria, December 1997

Song—A Source of Strength and Joy

The choir started to sing, "leh, leh, leh," in four-part harmony. Very softly, as through a haze, the first measures of Dvorak's "Largo" came floating through the [prison camp]. The music slowly swelled. . . . I felt a shiver go down my back. I thought I had never heard anything so beautiful before. . . . The music didn't sound like a woman's chorus singing songs. It didn't sound precisely like an orchestra either, although it was close. I could imagine I heard violins and an English horn. The music sounded ethereal, totally unreal in our sordid surroundings.

Each time we heard the music we marveled again at the beautiful and often familiar melodies, at the purity of sound, at this miracle that was happening to us amid the cockroaches, the rats, the bed bugs, and the stink of the latrines. The music renewed our sense of human dignity.

Helen Colijn
Song of Survival: Women Interned

Small Moments

R aymond Waites describes life as "a mosaic of small moments . . . like the silhouette of a flower against a patterned wall." These are moments that involve the senses: taste, touch, smell, sound, and sight. It's the fragrance of fresh flowers and the cool feel of clean linen. The sound of a song wafting on the wind. These are simple pleasures that bring beauty into our lives.

What do you think of when you think of "small moments"?

    hearing a newborn baby cry

    smelling warm blackberry cobbler on the kitchen counter

    singing an old hymn in church

    walking down a pine-needled pathway

    roasting marshmallows over an open fire

_____

_____

_____

_____

_____

_____

LEARN TO LIKE PLAIN FOOD, PLAIN SERVICE, PLAIN COOKING.

Food is like a beautiful woman: It is sometimes more dramatic and more appealing when simply and honestly presented.

Pierre Bardiche

*E*verything now is so fast-paced, and people don't sit down together anymore for dinner. People need to remember what is important. It's families sharing what they have: their work, their food, their good times and bad, no matter how hard things get.

Vern Berry
Roots and Recipes

A Curly Apple Peel

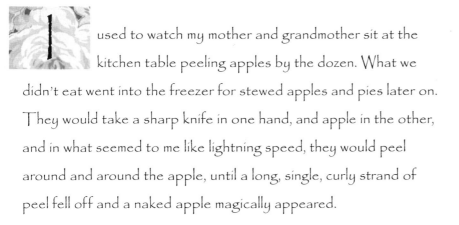

I used to watch my mother and grandmother sit at the kitchen table peeling apples by the dozen. What we didn't eat went into the freezer for stewed apples and pies later on. They would take a sharp knife in one hand, and apple in the other, and in what seemed to me like lightning speed, they would peel around and around the apple, until a long, single, curly strand of peel fell off and a naked apple magically appeared.

I was convinced that one of the rites of passage to womanhood in my household was to be able to peel an apple from stem to core without breaking the curl, and I practiced and practiced until I, too, could take my place at the harvest ritual. It was around the kitchen table that I first learned about family legends and about the facts of life, and it was here that I first experienced the joy of shared work and shared laughter.

Laura C. Martin
Handmade Gifts from a Country Garden

Many of us are drawn to our kitchens like birds to their nests. Of all the rooms in our lives, the kitchen can feed the soul and become a comforting place to be at any time of the day. I think of the kitchen as a gathering place, a place for shared comforts, for mutual efforts at preparing good meals with loving care. One's kitchen can become a place in which to confirm your love of life.

Alexandra Stoddard
Living a Beautiful Life

A pie is a simple thing...

In the country, farm folk reveled in the coming of spring. . . .
Women cleaned the storerooms and the potato and apple
houses to see what needed to be used before the growing season
began again. In the years of our childhood, Mama sorted the hard
Arkansas Black apples that had set in her closet from December
until spring. Daddy and Grandpa carried the burlap bags of apples
out into our kitchen, filling the entire house with their heady fruity
fragrance. Grandpa, who often helped, wanted Mama to make apple
pies, and Daddy, who loved turnovers drizzled with powdered-sugar
glaze, agreed to help peel the apples.

Jane Watson Hopping
The Pioneer Lady's Hearty Winter Cookbook

I first bought one of these pies at an autumn country church bazaar in North Carolina, and was soon telephoning through dozens of deacons, elders, and their wives to track down the recipe—which, thankfully, was given to me cheerfully and with hearty good wishes for happy eating.

Japanese Fruit Pie

Prepare your favorite pie crust and line a 9-inch pie tin.

Beat together:

- 2 eggs
- 1 cup sugar
- 1 tablespoon vinegar
- 1/2 cup raisins
- 1/2 cup melted butter

Add:

- 1/2 cup coconut
- 1/2 cup pecans

Pour into prepared crust and bake in a 300 degree oven for 40 minutes.

Cool and serve with a dollop of whipped cream. Enjoy!

T. G.

I remember Friday best—baking day. [Grandma Welty's] pies, enough for a week, were set to cool when done on the kitchen windowsills, side by side like so many cheeky faces telling us "One at a time!"

Eudora Welty

Sharing in the
Winter of 1950

Morning brought cold sunshine to light the white ice and snow-covered islands with sparkling brilliance. . . . The beauty . . . of the Finnish people [over the] next ten days, in sharing whatever there was to share, filled us with much emotion. Miss Anderson apologized for the fact that since the war, most Finns were eating only two meals a day. Breakfast consisted of porridge and milk, bread made with dark rye flour, a bit of cheese, a berry sauce something like jam but with very little sugar, and coffee. The next meal came at 4:00 p.m., with boiled potatoes, a small amount of meat or sausage or fish, and some pudding and coffee. Vegetables were almost nonexistent and too expensive for ordinary people. Beets ground up in vinegar sauce were the only vegetable we had during the ten days. But the Finnish people had nothing different after ten days, as they stayed on in the same situation!

Edith Schaeffer
The Tapestry

Little Touches That
Say so Much

I like Edward G. Dobson's advice: "Hold things loosely and give them away regularly." It's a way of keeping our lives a little less cluttered while being a good neighbor. What do you enjoy giving away? What do you enjoy receiving?

a homemade pie for a new neighbor

a letter or card for a loved one

hugs and kisses for grandkids

a potted cutting for a friend

_____

_____

_____

_____

_____

_____

_____

_____

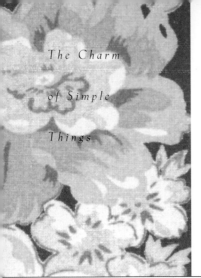

The Charm

of Simple

Things

The kiss of the sun

for pardon,

The song of the birds

for mirth—

One is nearer God's

heart in a garden

Than anywhere else

on earth.

Dorothy Frances Gurney

A garden is a simple thing...

W hat I love best about being surrounded by gardens—aside from the sheer beauty of them—is being able to go out and gather fresh things to enliven and beautify my life. It is my greatest joy to go out on our property and bring in an apron load of lemons, avocados, nectarines . . . or a basket of roses and lilies and some exuberant parsley and fragrant rosemary. The other day I even picked a few pansies to decorate a chocolate cake! . . .

And I have found that my garden is bountiful with gifts of all kinds. A little basket of potpourri makes a thoughtful housewarming gift. A preplanted herb garden with recipes or bottles of home-dried herbs will delight a newlywed couple. . . . With a little imagination, your garden becomes a cornucopia of gifts for every season.

Emilie Barnes
Secrets of the Garden

My Bountiful Garden

At about seven or eight o'clock in the evening, I love to walk in the vegetable garden. I always feel my grandfather's spirit is there among the lush plants, the lavender and purple eggplant bushes, and the deep green pepper plants, with their hanging globes, thick-meated and sweet to the taste. . . . The corn won't be ready for harvest until later, but the silk is as soft as a woman's hair, and the ears become fuller almost day by day. . . . As dusk comes on and shadows fall, and the air gets cool, I wander back toward the house, taking with me a sense of having been in touch with all that is fragile and yet bountiful, all that sustains us.

Jane Watson Hopping
The Lazy Days of Summer Cookbook

We had seven weeks of this "normal life" during which the excitement of digging up and planting the vegetable garden in the front yard took place. The seeds had come from Burpee's in Philadelphia, and nothing could match the wonder of seeing the variety of green shoots come up in that garden in the Swiss Alps except the wonder of eating the crop a few months later.

Edith Schaeffer
The Tapestry

Soup is a simple thing...

For simple living, when one is alone or with children or other people who must sleep sweetly and then rise to face school or jobs, the supper of our European forebears is a good one, and when one feels jaded from too many pressures it seems even more beneficent: all one wants to eat of a plain soup, some bread or toast, perhaps, then a compote of cooked fruits or a little custard if indicated by habit or hunger, and then bed.

M. F. K. Fisher
With Bold Knife and Fork

Huge pots of stock made from bones, trimming and the cooking water from vegetables, simmered all day long and were used for nourishing soups—creamy chowders, smooth vegetable soups, broths with rice, and clear soups with vegetables and herbs. In the early days, soup often formed the main part of the meal at supper, with bread and butter, cheese and stewed fruit.

Norma MacMillan
In a Shaker Kitchen

Portuguese Potato Soup

12 cups chicken or vegetable broth (or 12 cups water and one
   bouillon cube)

3 or 4 large potatoes (peeled and cubed)

1 or 2 cloves garlic

1 bunch collards (washed well, drained, bunched together and
   sliced very fine)

16 ounces kielbasa sausage (skin removed and cubed)

2 egg yolks

3/4 cup half-and-half

salt and pepper to taste

In a large sauce pan bring broth, garlic, and potatoes to a boil. Reduce
heat and simmer until potatoes are tender. Remove pan from stove and
beat mixture with an electric mixer until smooth. Add collards and
kielbasa. Return to heat. Simmer over medium heat 10–15 minutes,
until collards are tender.

Beat egg yolks and combine with half-and-half. When collards are
tender, remove soup from heat and gradually add yolk mixture. Season
to taste.

Serve piping hot with parmesan toast. Que gostoso!

T. G.

> *Blessed shall be your basket*
> *and your kneading bowl.*
>
> **Deuteronomy 28:5**

Simply Serendipitous

Happiness is not a right to be grasped, but a serendipity to be enjoyed.

Richard J. Foster

sn't it fun when a simple, spontaneous pleasure suddenly interrupts our busy schedule? It's a happiness that comes on us suddenly, like the surprise of a butterfly in a winter woods—a memorable moment of serendipity.

Can you think of a few that have happened to you?

receiving a romantic letter from your true love

enjoying a barbecue with dear out-of-town friends

a first rose blooming in the garden

finding a special antique at a tag sale

_____

_____

_____

_____

_____

_____

LEARN TO LIKE PEOPLE, EVEN THOSE WHO MAY BE VERY DIFFERENT FROM YOU.

LEARN TO SHELTER YOUR FAMILY WITH LOVE, COMFORT, AND PEACE.

Don't worry about having things. Worry about having each other.

Diane Rosoener

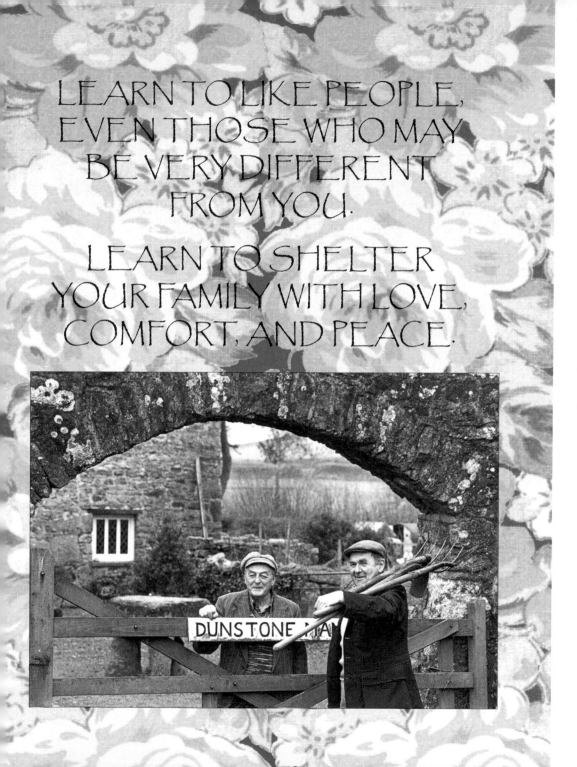

The ornament of a
house is the friends
who frequent it.

Ralph
Waldo
Emerson

Kindness is a simple thing...

Little acts of kindness that we render to each other in everyday life, are like flowers by the way-side to the traveler:
they serve to gladden the heart and relieve the tedium of life's journey.

Eunice Bathrick

Speak gently,—it is better far
To rule by love than fear;
Speak gently,—let not harsh words mar
The good we might do here. . . .

Speak gently, 'tis a little thing
Dropp'd in the heart's deep well;
The good, the joy which it may bring,
Eternity shall tell.

Anonymous

Kindness Sows Seeds of Love

I think there is something wonderful about everyone, and whenever I get the opportunity to tell someone this, I do.

Mary Kay

Do not waste time bothering whether you "love" your neighbor; act as if you did. As soon as we do this we find one of the great secrets. When you are behaving as if you loved someone, you will presently come to love him.

C. S. Lewis

It's true. When we do others a good turn, even if they have not done so to us, we find ourselves liking them more and more with every act of kindness. And what are good deeds for, if not for giving away? Add a few more to the list when you think of them.

read with a child snuggled in bed

spend time over afternoon tea with a friend

take a puppy along to visit a shut-in

mail homemade goodies to a college student

_____

_____

_____

_____

_____

_____

_____

_____

_____

Near and Dear

O ur old folk have a gentle acceptance of life as it is and has been—an acceptance that seems to flow from some inner placid pool. They have a soft, loving way with the little ones that promises them a life worth living. Through their actions, the elders share the belief that our children are the future.

All the younger folk in the family have the same respect for the elderly. When my father grew older, Mother, Sheila, and I intuitively knew that some of his strength and character had become ours. We were content when he didn't do anything other than sit in his chair and doze. His presence was enough.

Jane Watson Hopping
The Pioneer Lady's Hearty Winter Cookbook

Where will the kind, thoughtful, caring people come from for the next generation if our children are not taught the value of putting someone else's needs above their own?

Edith Schaeffer

*f I can stop one heart
from breaking,
I shall not live in vain;
If I can ease one life the aching,
Or cool one pain,
Or help one fainting robin
Unto his nest again,
I shall not live in vain.*

Emily Dickinson

Friendship is a simple thing...

Often the deepest relationships can be developed during the simplest activities.

Gary Smalley

My house must have a door so I can enter myself, and a window so I can see beyond myself.

Noah benShea

Anyone who has ever attended a college reunion knows how easily two friends who haven't seen each other for years can pick up the thread of a conversation as if they had just flung it down, like a skirt they had been hemming, to answer the doorbell.

Phyllis Theroux

Money Can't Buy It

L ove is something like the clouds that were in the sky before the sun came out," [my teacher] replied. "You cannot touch the clouds, you know; but you feel the rain and know how glad the flowers and the thirsty earth are to have it after a hot day. You cannot touch love either; but you feel the sweetness that it pours into everything."

Helen Keller
The Story of My Life

Instead of a gem, or even a flower, if we could cast the gift of a lovely thought into the heart of a friend, that would be giving as the angels give.

George MacDonald

Teatime is a simple thing...

In the clear light of a winter's day, the Luberon becomes a magnificent array of grays, blues and yellows. If you go for a brisk walk in the afternoon you can work up a warming glow, but as soon as the sun dips down behind the hills, you have to retreat back home.

On your return , having hung the coats and scarves in the hallway . . . you can take refuge in the kitchen, warmed by a bright burning fire and smelling exquisitely of sugar, butter, and vanilla. With rosy cheeks and eyes bright with expectation, everyone is ready for a delicious afternoon tea. On the long wooden table covered with a linen cloth are bowls and cups, a large pot of dark, thick steamy hot chocolate, a pitcher of warm milk, a slab of sweet butter, some delicious slices of country bread, a selection of cheeses and jams.

Michel Biehn
Recipes from a Provençal Kitchen

Store sugar cubes for tea in a jar with whole cloves or cinnamon sticks. They will absorb the spicy fragrance.

Maggie Stuckey

A Tea Party Is
Always in Season

We set the long pine harvest table . . . with a brown bowl of spring flowers; with brown-and-white china with which Mother started housekeeping. . . . Fill the copper teakettle on the summer-kitchen stove and bring it just to the boil; take from the oven the pans of gingerbread. Serve the hot and fragrant spicy tea from an old Bennington teapot, and enjoy a country tea party in the spring. . . .

On a sunny summer's day, the place for an afternoon tea party . . . is in the arbor. It is shaded by an ancient grapevine, dripping with fuchsias in hanging baskets, and lined with potted geraniums. The ice-cream table is covered with a gay checked cloth; spoons and tea knives are in a basket. We fill a cut-glass pitcher with minted iced tea. A bowl of raspberries or strawberries or blackberries, picked with the hulls left on, is ready for dipping one by one into superfine sugar. . . .

In the winter, tea is served in the best parlor with the warmth of a hearth-fire to take the chill off the leafless look of the garden and the sleet singing against the windowpanes. Favorite friends come in for visits and so the Canton cups are taken from the shelf, and the spirit lamp is lighted under the silver teakettle. . . . Here in our favorite chairs with a warm hooked rug under our feet . . . we savor the tea and the moments.

Mary Mason Campbell
The New England Butt'ry Shelf Cookbook

Tante Claire's
Apple Tarte

1 3/4 cups flour

1 1/2 cups sugar

1/2 teaspoon salt

1/4 teaspoon baking powder

3/4 cup butter

3/4 teaspoon cinnamon

1/4 teaspoon nutmeg

2 egg yolks

1 cup heavy cream

1 teaspoon vanilla

4 apples, peeled, cored, cut in thin slices

Preheat oven to 375 degrees and butter a 9-inch, round baking pan.

Combine flour, 1 cup sugar, salt, and baking powder. With pastry blender, cut in butter. Turn mixture into pan and pat firmly on sides and bottom.

Arrange apple slices over batter. Sprinkle with a mixture of the remaining sugar, nutmeg, and cinnamon.

Bake 15 minutes. Remove from oven.

Beat egg yolks with cream and vanilla. Pour over the apples.

Bake for another 25 minutes. Let stand 10 minutes and serve. Trés bien!

T. G.

> *There are few hours in life more agreeable than the hour dedicated to the ceremony known as afternoon tea.*
>
> **Henry James**

A precious family is a simple thing...

On wet, rainy days in spring, women in our families got together to plan large family potlucks. They were sure to invite all their old friends. . . . Men and boys talked the women into making large pots of soup and pans of hot corn bread. Sometimes women and girls made a raisin pie or a batch of oatmeal cookies.

Most often, meals were simple. Families brought whatever they had to share: simple pots of beans with or without meat in them, split peas, and mashed, scalloped, and baked potatoes. Some brought home-canned tomatoes and fruit.

Jane Watson Hopping
The Pioneer Lady's Hearty Winter Cookbook

The family is the principal setting for learning ordinary, decent behavior.

Mary Ann Glendon

Learning stamps you with its moments. Childhood's learning is made up of moments. It isn't steady. It's a pulse.

Eudora Welty

Speaking of Love

The last time [I was able to visit my dear old friends] Alwine and Franzle. . .I spent the last Christmas of their life with them and the crowd of children and adults that were our family. What a lovely ritual. Near the big chimney was a huge Christmas tree full of little wooden hand-cut objects and real candles burning fiercely. At eight o'clock Alwine's son Hansi read the story of the Nativity and we all sang Christmas carols in German. Everyone gave presents, and mine was precious. It was a package containing [my Grandmother's] diary and her cook book, both in her own hand, written in German.

Madeleine Kamman
When French Women Cook

Don't miss love. It's an incredible gift. I love to think that the day you're born, you're given the world as your birthday present. It frightens me that so few people even bother to open up the ribbon! Rip it open! Tear off the top! It's just full of love and magic and life and joy and wonder and pain and tears.

Leo Buscaglia

A Family Album

Home is where we return

for fulfillment and

wholeness.

Alexdandra Stoddard

Heaven is along the way.

Catherine of Siena

Teaching Values and Virtues

You can't teach good character if you don't live it.

Tom Lickona

Mother's rules for guidance—

    Rule yourself.

    Love your neighbor.

    Do the duty which

        lies nearest you.

Louisa May Alcott

We can teach our children values and virtues by the way we live, because how we spend our time speaks to our children about what we hold dear. In a day when money and materialism often seem more important than honesty and compassion, our children need our help if they are going to become good citizens. What would you add to this list?

To encourage reading—read aloud to your children and provide plenty of books.

To encourage physical fitness—walk, and run, and skip with them.

To encourage a love of church—take them regularly.

_____

_____

_____

_____

_____

_____

_____

_____

A Mother's Reward

Doris paused on her way downstairs. Jon and Joe were standing looking at the freshly cut Christmas tree as it stood in the living room. Doris watched them—just two little boys of five and four with rumpled hair and faded overalls. Lost in dreaming of glowing lights and gay, mysterious packages, they had not heard [her] step upon the stairs. They talked together in low voices as [she] watched and waited. Suddenly Jon bowed his head and prayed, "Dear Lord, we love Thee, Amen." Joe followed his example, "Dear Lord, I love Thee, A-man." Her heart swelled in gratitude to the Lord for the love her small sons had expressed so spontaneously. How rewarding it was for all her training and care!

**Belva Atkinson
Murphy**
*Mommie of the
Mixing Bowl*

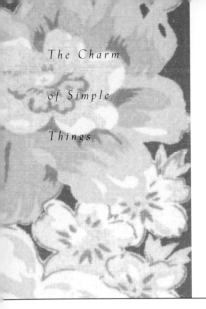

> *"I do think that families are
> the most beautiful things in
> all the world!"*
>
> **Jo Marsh**
> in *Little Women*

The Simple Pleasures
of the Hour

There were a great many holidays at Plumfield, and one of the most delightful was the yearly apple-picking.... The old orchard wore its holiday attire; golden-rod and asters fringed the mossy walls; grasshoppers skipped briskly in the sere grass, and crickets chirped like fairy pipers at a feast....

Jo and Meg, with a detachment of the bigger boys, set forth the supper on the grass, for an out-of-door tea was always the crowning joy of the day. The land literally flowed with milk and honey on such occasions, for the lads were not required to sit at table, but allowed to partake of refreshment as they liked—freedom being the sauce best beloved by the boyish soul. They availed themselves of the rare privilege to the fullest extent, for some tried the pleasing experiment of drinking milk while standing on their heads, others lent a charm to leap-frog by eating pie in the pauses of the game; cookies were sown broadcast over the field, and apple turnovers roosted in the trees like a new style of bird.

Louisa May Alcott
Little Women

A picnic is a simple thing...

What a heavenly day to be on the mountain! Sparkling-clear. What fun it is to climb to the top through the shade of the forest where we find ferns and mosses and the patches of shiny green and Christmas red bunch berry. Stumble over the big rocks, skip around the slippery places where a mountain spring bubbles, jump over trees fallen in the great hurricane of 1938. Suddenly we are out in the brilliant sunshine with only the blue of the sky above and around us. We have left the forest behind and are standing on a rock ledge at the very top. Our view of the world below takes our breath away.

The picnic table is laden. . . . Hot soup is poured from the thermos into blue granite cups. . . . Tomatoes and cucumbers are sliced into a bowl and then dusted with fresh tarragon—help yourself. Tear off a piece of warm French bread with garlic butter. . . . Finally the pie basket is opened and green-apple pie is cut in wide pieces . . . Pour steaming coffee from the pot on the fire or have a cup of fresh milk.

After the dinner is over . . . we sit on the rocks and visit. . . . We watch the evening haze spread as the sun sets over the land below.

Mary Mason Campbell
The New England Butt'ry Shelf Cookbook

A picnic is a time to escape totally from the normal family routine: no dining room, no set places at the table, and hands, rather than forks, are used to pick up the food. Even when a column of ants marches across the tablecloth, we sit back and, slightly bemused, we watch them walk on by.

Michel Biehn
Recipes from a Provençal Kitchen

Picnic Pasta Salad

salad:

> 2 cups elbow macaroni, cooked and drained
>
> 1/4 cup chopped olives (green or nicoise)
>
> 1/2 chopped tomatoes
>
> 1 cup green beans cooked al dente and chopped
>
> 1/4 cup chopped green onions

Combine the salad ingredients and sprinkle with kosher salt and freshly ground pepper to taste. (Feel free to adjust proportions of ingredients according to your liking.)

dressing:

> 1 teaspoon Dijon mustard
>
> 1 tablespoon wine vinegar
>
> 1/2 cup olive oil

Whisk mustard and vinegar. Slowly add olive oil. Pour over salad and mix well. Sprinkle with freshly grated parmesan cheese. Cover tightly and enjoy along with your other picnic fixing's.

T. G.

*I want to feel little, more
simple, more mild,
More like our blest parents,
and more like a child,
More thankful, more humble,
more lowly in mind
More watchful, more pray'rful,
more loving and kind.*

Anonymous

The Nest of Childhood

Although I'm not sure she realized it at the time, my mother believed in creating memories for her daughters—a perfect morning, a glimpse of winter stars—bright pebbles to carry from the nest of childhood. It was her way of defining what she thought should matter to us. She wanted her children to love the world sensually, as she did, and to appreciate small, homely adventures. She also believed in participating in any adventure she charted out—wading barefoot in a creek hunting for crawfish, for instance. I can still recall the cool ooze of mud between my toes, the warmth of the sun on the back of my neck, and my mother, her linen skirt bunched around her knees, wading beside me, laughing at the leaf shadows dappling the water.

Suzanne Berne
Victoria, May 1996

LEARN TO KEEP YOUR WANTS SIMPLE. REFUSE TO BE OWNED AND ANCHORED BY THINGS AND OPINIONS OF OTHERS.

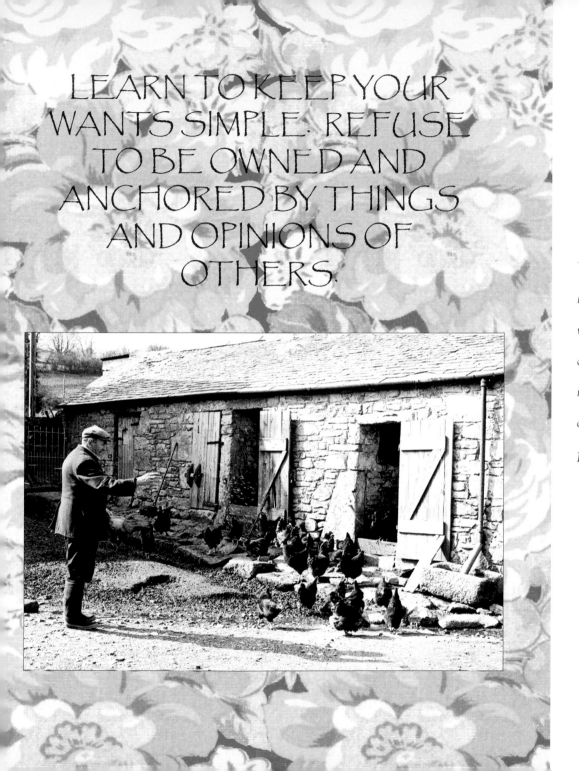

We are usually so busily longing for things we can't have that we overlook what we have in their place that is even more worthwhile.

Laura Ingalls Wilder

Today more of us in America than anywhere else in the world have the luxury of choice between simplicity and complication of life. And for the most part, we, who could choose simplicity, choose complication.

Anne Morrow Lindbergh

Enough Is a Feast

Most of us tend to bite off much more than we can chew in life. And because we cannot chew what we have bitten off, we tend to take life in lumps and have difficulty digesting it at all.

Too many of us take on too much. We are overly ambitious, overly acquisitive, overly possessive. We are much better off to take just a little of anything at a time, taste it fully, and suck all the sweetness from it. "Enough is a feast."

W. Phillip Keller
Taming Tension

Money, we imagine, offers the freedom, contentment, and respect we crave. Spending it, we discover that what was new and better is soon old and inferior. To stay in the race, it's soon time for another purchase, time to discard what we haven't long possessed. Rather than acting of our own free will, we're making passive, predictable decisions. Rather than being comfortable with what we own and who we are, we become restless captives to a vicious cycle of earning enough bucks to buy what we think we want.

Frank Levering and Wanda Urbanska
Simple Living

Refreshed by Simplicity

There is something about baking bread that brings me back to earth from all the stresses of everyday modern life. Maybe it's kneading the dough, in all its simplicity and physicalness, that helps the most in relaxing me. Maybe it's the time required to let the bread rise that forces me temporarily to slow down. But whatever it is, these "back to earth days" and baking bread in general have become for me a safety zone where I can take some time and gain a perspective on what I'm doing. It is as though my feet get firmly placed again on earth, and the problems of yesterday begin to look solvable. Afterwards, that which looked hopeless no longer seems so impossible, and that which seemed complex appears less so in the light of a new day.

Elizabeth Skoglund
A Quiet Courage

Contentment is
a simple thing...

There are so many little heedless ways in which a few cents are wasted here and a few more there. The total would be truly surprising if we should sum them up. I illustrated this to myself in an odd way lately. While looking over the pages of a catalog advertising articles from two cents to ten cents, [my husband] said, "There are a good many little [things] you'd like to have. Get what you want; they will only cost a few cents." So, I made out a list of what I wanted, things I decided I could not get along without as I found them, one by one, on those alluring pages. I was surprised when I added up the cost to find that it amounted to five dollars. I put the list away intending to go over it and cut out some things to make the total less. That was several months ago, and I have not yet missed any of the things I would have ordered. I have decided to let the list wait until I do.

Laura Ingalls Wilder
Saving Graces

> Many people buy what they want, when they want, so they will not want. But the truth is that much of what they buy they do not want.
>
> *Edward G. Dobson*

*W*ho has not found the
heaven below
Will fail of it above.
God's residence is next to mine,
His furniture is love.

Emily Dickinson

Material Minutia

Our attention is continually grabbed by the minutia of our lives. Even the choice of donuts (chocolate, cake, glazed, sprinkled, blueberry, long johns, bear claws, etc., etc., etc.) becomes a big event. Just to get through the grocery store requires diligent attention to brands, prices, labels, fat content, calories, while competing ads echo in our minds. Trivia. Even deciding what to wear is sometimes a problem, changing from aerobics, to work, to at-home, to evening clothes all in one day. Exhausting. . . .

Our culture seems to demand focus on materiality, while our souls are starving. Just getting along from day to day, we seem to become covered with the pitch of the world, and like tar, materialism is difficult to get rid of. We walk around getting stuck to things that are not important to our salvation.

Leslie Williams
Night Wrestling

A Simple and Orderly Life

Use it up, wear it out;

make it do, or do

without.

New England Proverb

Simplifying life is about balance, about getting control of your life. You don't have to escape to the woods to simplify your life. Changing your lifestyle doesn't have to involve only drastic things. Even small changes help—like paring down and acquiring less. Here are some ways to simplify life. What would simplify your life?

clean out your closets and drawers

give away clothing you haven't used in the past year

retire from at least one committee

buy one type of cereal instead of four

decide on two attractive colors of lipstick, get rid of the other six

_____

_____

_____

_____

_____

_____

_____

_____

The Cornerstone
of Contentment

There are two ways to get enough," G. K. Chesterton once said. "One is to continue to accumulate more and more and the other is to desire less." Giving is like an inverted savings program: We find as we participate in giving that God shrinks our mercenary desires. Giving tames our lusts.

"Godliness with contentment is great gain" (1 Tim. 6:6, NIV). It is the freedom to concentrate on more important things, the ability to say, "This is enough. I don't need one more winter sweater, one more kitchen gadget, or fifty more feet of lawn to mow."

Stacy and Paula Rinehart
Living in Light of Eternity

> *We can choose to be rich by*
> *making our wants few.*
> **Alexandra Stoddard**

An uncluttered life is a simple thing...

One way to simplify life is to make it less cluttered and thus less complicated.

Make a list of some things that clutter your life. Include activities, lifestyle habits, relationships, employment, etc. Now go through the list and cross off all the things you can change immediately or eliminate. Go back through the list a second time and mark things that could be eliminated or changed with more effort.

Here are some you might not have thought of:

phone calls
junk mail
television

_____

_____

_____

_____

_____

One cannot collect all the beautiful shells on the beach. One can collect only a few, and they are more beautiful if they are few.

Anne Morrow Lindbergh

Help Me to Unclutter My Life, Lord

Rescue me from this eternal confusion of belongings (mine and other people's) that just won't stay orderly. This suffocation of phone calls, clubs and committees. . . This choke of bills and papers and magazines and junk mail. I buy too many things, subscribe to too many things, belong to too many things. The result is such confusion I can't really enjoy or do justice to anything!

Deliver me from some of this Lord. Help me to stop bewailing this clutter and work out some plan for cutting down.

Give me the will power to stop buying things we don't really need. . . . And give, oh give me the will power to get rid of a lot of things we already have. . . .And while I'm at it Lord, help me to unclutter my mind. Of regrets and resentments and anxieties, of idiotic dialogues and foolish broodings.

Sweep it clean and free.

Make it calm and quiet.

Make it orderly.

Marjorie Holmes
Lord Let Me Love

An everyday blessing
is a simple thing...

As the years pass, I am coming more and more to understand that it is the common, everyday blessings of our common everyday lives for which we should be particularly grateful. They are the things that fill our lives with comfort and our hearts with gladness—just the pure air to breathe and the strength to breathe it; just warmth and shelter and home folks; just plain food that gives us strength; the bright sunshine on a cold day; and a cool breeze when the day is warm.

Laura Ingalls Wilder
Saving Graces

Back to Essential Things

Storms had cut off the electricity, and telephone wires were down. The children enjoyed the novelty of the situation. At night the soft glow of the shiny kerosene lamp left the family room in mysterious shadows. The roaring fire felt the warmer because of the whiteness and cold outside.

Mommie cooked over the fireplace. The children enjoyed the pot roast browned and cooked along with the potatoes in the old, three-legged black iron kettle. The breakfast toast had a smoky flavor that seemed far better than the usual oven variety. And the coffee pot on the hearth added a cheerful note. . . .

In the evenings the family gathered around the fireside for a time of prayer. The lamplight cast a soft glow on the paneled walls and the firelight shone softly on the children's faces. . . . Somehow it did seem that we were back to the essential things—warmth, shelter, the fireside, the glow of lamps and candles, and the large pan of snow melting on the hearth.

Doris Aldrich Coffin
in *Mommie of the Mixing Bowl*

*T*each us to delight in
simple things,
And mirth that has no
bitter springs;
Forgiveness free of evil
done,
And love to all men
'neath the sun!

Rudyard Kipling
(1865–1936)

Enjoy Simple, Spontaneous Pleasures

Harriet Crosby said there is only one rule to practicing simplicity—keep it simple. When we do keep life simple we have more time to enjoy spontaneous pleasures. Here are some of my suggestions. Add your own *after* you have taken time out to enjoy them (no fair cheating).

> plan next summer's flower garden from seed catalogs
>
> walk the dog through an open meadow
>
> savor a thermos of hot tea in the shelter of a beach dune
>
> on a brisk day
>
> refurbish a flea market find
>
> read a book to a child

Getting things accomplished isn't nearly as important as taking time for love.

Janette Oke

_____

_____

_____

_____

_____

_____

_____

The Delight of Simple Things

In the center of this little hamlet was Victoire's house. It was an old stone building, southern in style with a round tiled roof and an enormous grapevine climbing up all the way under the eaves. As we entered . . . all I could do was stand there looking, my eyes opening wider and wider, at a world that I had no idea existed. There was a huge chimney, black with the smoke of centuries in which a pine needle and wood fire burned bright. And something mysterious, something I had never seen before—a bread oven. . . . On the table were three huge loaves of dark bread, their fresh smell still permeating the atmosphere. The bread paddles used to send the loaves to bake in the depths of the oven were hanging above the mantel. There was a table covered with an electric blue and white checkered tablecloth loaded with fresh bread slices, butter, rich and yellow, a side of bacon, several [sausages], and a huge pot of café au lait.

Madeleine Kamman
When French Women Cook

LEARN TO LIKE THE SUNRISE
AND THE SUNSET,

THE BEATING OF RAIN ON
THE ROOF AND WINDOWS,

THE GENTLE FALL OF
SNOW IN WINTER.

The one who walks

through a countryside

sees much more than

the one who runs.

Anonymous

*In winter,
when the world is
simplified, the subtler
and humbler beauties
can appear to us. . . .
Red holly berries, or
rose hips on their dry
canes. . . . Even a
blue jay stands out.
The simplicity and
starkness of a winter
scene bring to our
attention creatures
we overlook in other
seasons. The beauty
of such small and
humble things is an
especially important
expression of holiness
for us, who are so
easily impressed
by size and ostentation.*

David Rensberger

God's beautiful earth
is a simple thing...

A s we go about our daily tasks, the work will seem lighter if
we enjoy the beautiful things that are just outside our
doors and windows. It pays to go to the top of the hill now and then
to see the view and to stroll thru the woodlot or
pasture, forgetting that we are in a hurry
or that there is such a thing as a clock
in the world. . . . We are all
busy, but what are we
living for anyway, and
why is the world so
beautiful if not for
us? . . . Let's not make
such a habit of hurry and work that when we leave this world, we will
feel impelled to hurry through the spaces of the universe using our
wings for feather dusters to clean away the star dust.

Laura Ingalls Wilder
Saving Graces

Live Gently

Throughout our rural areas, there are old abandoned farmsteads that cling to the earth. Near barns and outbuildings, delicate crocuses thrust their heads through ice and snow to charm those who pass by. Great beds of them show off their multiplied beauty. Sometimes they share a spot with richly colored grape hyacinths. Violets throw their white, pink, lavender, and magenta blankets at the feet of ancient maple trees.

Jane Watson Hopping

People have to know what relaxes them, and not feel guilty about using a piece of time when it is necessary for them, or when they do not use it exactly as somebody else would.

Edith Schaeffer

Taking Time for Sunshine and Laughter

The out-of-doors is a great place to relive adorable childhood memories, to become like children again who thrive on simple pleasures. What a perfect way to renew our spirits and invigorate our hearts. What would be some of your favorites?

walk barefoot through a creek

fly a kite

hold a baby chick

jump onto a haystack

_____

_____

_____

_____

_____

_____

_____

_____

Holiness in Hidden Places

W hat does it mean to become simple? I think of the abbey of New Mellary in Iowa, the walls of its church long plastered over, until the architectural consultant the monks had hired to help them remodel discovered that underneath the plaster were walls of native stone. The monks themselves did the work of uncovering them, and now the church is a place where one can sit and wait and watch the play of sunlight and shadow, a place made holy by the simple glory of light on stone.

What would I find in my own heart if the noise of the world were silenced?

Kathleen Norris
The Cloister Walk

Where there is no time for quiet, there is no time for the soul to grow.

Anonymous

We like this quiet little place among the mountains, and pass lazy days; for it is very warm, and we sit about on our balconies enjoying the soft air, the moonlight, and the changing aspect of the hills.

Louisa May Alcott

The gift of time is a simple thing...

In our culture, time can seem like an enemy: it chews us up and spits us out with appalling ease. But the monastic perspective welcomes time as a gift from God, and seeks to put it to good use rather than allowing us to be used up by it. A friend who was educated by the Benedictines has told me that she owes to them her sanity with regard to time. "You never really finish anything in life," she says, "and while that's humbling, and frustrating, it's all right. The Benedictines . . . insist that there is time in each day for prayer, for work, for study, and for play." Liturgical time is essentially poetic time, oriented toward process rather than productivity, willing to wait attentively in stillness rather than always pushing to "get the job done."

Kathleen Norris, *The Cloister Walk*

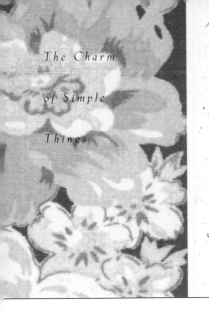

> *The heart which has no*
> *agenda but God's is*
> *the heart at leisure*
> *from itself.*
>
> **Elisabeth Elliot**

A Pattern of Balance

istraction is, always has been, and probably always will be, inherent in woman's life.

For to be a woman is to have interests and duties, raying out in all directions from the central mother-core, like spokes from the hub of a wheel. The pattern of our lives is essentially circular. We must be open to all points of the compass; husband, children, friends, home, community; stretched out, exposed, sensitive like a spider's web to each breeze that blows, to each call that comes. How difficult for us, then, to achieve a balance in the midst of these contradictory tensions, and yet how necessary for the proper functioning of our lives.

Anne Morrow Lindbergh
Gift from the Sea

A List for Simplifying Life

1. Drop useless goals. You may be wearing yourself out doing things that do not matter.

2. Don't try to do it all yourself. Leave some of the world's building to others.

3. Live one day at a time. Live this day well and tomorrow's strength will come.

4. Enjoy what you are doing while you're doing it. Learn to live in the present.

5. Develop a hobby. Time spent at play is time well spent.

6. If it is impossible to slow your world down, slow yourself down. When you can't alter the whirling pace, retire to your inner sanctuary and alter yourself.

7. Adopt the perfect pattern, which is Christ. Study him as he lives a life in quiet confidence.

Charlie Shedd
How to Make People Really Feel Loved

Take Time to Play Games and Read Stories

A balanced perspective reminds me that money does have its limitations. It can buy clothes but not true beauty. An exotic vacation but not the ability to relax and sleep. A big house but not a happy family. Sports fees and equipment but not a dad. Expensive gifts but not love. A Better Homes and Gardens lifestyle, but not a mom who has time and energy left to play games or read stories.

A balanced perspective also keeps me from being consumed by my desires and warns me about sacrificing what really matters in life for things that never quite satisfy. Contrary to the myth of materialism, it isn't the ones who die with the most toys who win. It's those who've loved their families well and know the joy of having that love returned. It's those who've known what it is to spend their lives for a purpose greater than themselves. It's those who've known their God and look forward to eternity with him.

Ruth Haley Barton
"In a Material World"

The Treasure of
Time Well-Spent

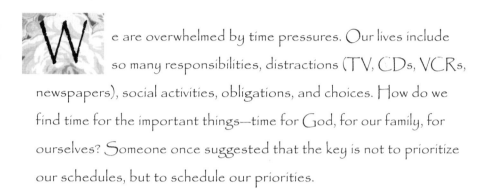

We are overwhelmed by time pressures. Our lives include so many responsibilities, distractions (TV, CDs, VCRs, newspapers), social activities, obligations, and choices. How do we find time for the important things—time for God, for our family, for ourselves? Someone once suggested that the key is not to prioritize our schedules, but to schedule our priorities.

Make a note here of days and events when you make an special effort to enjoy priority time with God, your family, and in private retreat. Then note the benefits you gain.

Every person, especially every woman, should be alone sometime during the year, some part of each week, and each day.

Anne Morrow Lindbergh

Date	How time was spent	Benefits gained

For warmth and love and tenderness,
For restful nights, for joyous days,
For all Thy love has given us;
We offer praise.

Doris Coffin Aldrich

Exclamation Marks in Ordinary Days

Make a list of things you would like to do if you had more time in your life—things you would love and enjoy doing (not what you should or ought to do but what you truly want to do). Put these in order of priority and pick the top five as goals to fulfill in the immediate future.

_____

_____

_____

_____

_____

_____

_____

_____

_____

_____

_____

_____

_____

_____

Time cannot be used over again. Time cannot be taken to the cleaners and brought back as good as new, to be used in another way. The use of time is a very permanent thing. . . . Time moves from the present tense into the past tense very relentlessly . . . a minute, an hour, a day, a week, a year, nine years! There it is. Childhood cannot be used over again for another set of preparations nor a different set of memories.

Edith Schaeffer
Common Sense Christian Living

The fathers of the Church well understood the importance of what they called otium sanctum (holy leisure). They knew that we cannot give ourselves to spiritual things and deepen our relationship with [God] if we are obsessed with a multitude of things to do and always on the go. Love for God is a tender plant that can mature only when it has time to grow. God cannot be loved on the run.

David Roper
A Man to Match the Mountain

LEARN TO HOLD HEAVEN NEAR AND DEAR.

LEARN TO LOVE GOD, FOR HE SURELY LOVES YOU.

There is no event so commonplace but that God is present within it.

Frederick Buechner

If we train ourselves, we can sense God's presence in every object or person we encounter during even a humdrum day; and recognizing the sparkle in the bubble is itself a way to worship the God who created bubbles and added sparkles for the fun of it.

Leslie Williams
Night Wrestling

Satisfying work
is a simple thing...

 **C**hildren don't build sand castles in order to take pictures of them or in hopes of winning a cash award. They build sand castles just for the pleasure of the process. My little nephew Jake didn't want to mow the lawn so he could stand back and observe a manicured yard. He just wanted the pleasure of pushing the mower.

Adults value the results. Children values the means. . . .

For a chance at childhood again, we must learn to value the process of work as well as the product. Our work, like our lives, must be redeemed.

Work needn't be a drudgery.

Alan D. Wright
A Chance at Childhood Again

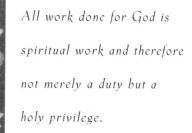

All work done for God is
spiritual work and therefore
not merely a duty but a
holy privilege.

Elisabeth Elliot

My Wonderful, Silly Work

It's hard to work today because autumn is so persistent about getting my attention. The birds and squirrels are busy making provision for winter, the first fire of the season keeps flickering and crackling to catch my eye and ear, the beech trees keep whispering about changing into their new fall fashions of gold, and the chestnuts keep dropping to the ground, making their own disturbance.

Even the air refuses to be sedate and quiet, but keeps sneaking around the corner of the porch, breathing nippy puffs at the back of my neck, only to pretend stillness when I turn to catch it at its game. A splash of red catches my eye, too. A black-and-white woodpecker tips his head to me in hopes that I will leave my silly work and join the celebration in the woods.

So how can I waste this day writing . . . and keep my good conscience? Should I squander this moment now and make a mockery of my intentions?

Gloria Gaither
We Have This Moment

A Christ-centered life—even in the midst of work—stays basically simple, nourished, and rested.

Anne Ortlund

Behind much of the rat-race of modern life is the unexamined assumption that what I do determines who I am. In this way, we define ourselves by what we do, rather than by any quality of what we are inside. It is typical in a party for one stranger to approach another with the question, "What do you do?" Perhaps we wouldn't have a clue how to reply to the deeper question, "Who are you?"

James Houston

I am in the garret with my paper round me, and a pile of apples to eat while I write my journal, plan stories, and enjoy the patter of rain on the roof, in peace and quiet.

Louisa May Alcott

The Little Things in Life

F ind moments to celebrate every day, especially on work days. How easy it is to forget that the little things in life turn out to be the important things. What ways of celebrating would you add to the list?

keep one fresh flower on your desk

listen to music on your lunch hour

read a chapter in a good book

plant herbs in a pot for your porch

relax in a warm herbal bath at the end of the day

If you have time to open the back door in the morning while you're drinking your coffee and look at the sky or hear the chorus the birds offer, you have time for the marvelous. You may only have a moment before the polite chaos of the day starts, but that moment can stretch to the horizon.

Diane Ackerman

Sabbath rest
is a simple thing...

W e've blown the whistle on ourselves. "Time out," we've declared. Time out to write letters. Time to sit on the porch watching the sun go down, enjoying time. Time to visit with Sam and Miriam at midmorning or linger with the newspaper after lunch. To cook from scratch, to tend our two woodstoves, to make our beds in the mornings and clean our house on Saturdays. The simple sorts of things that unfrazzled people do.

Along with our new attitude has come new ground rules: Sunday is a day of rest.

**Frank Levering
and Wanda Urbanska**
Simple Living

It takes about six days of work to give just the right flavor to a day off.

Laura Ingalls Wilder

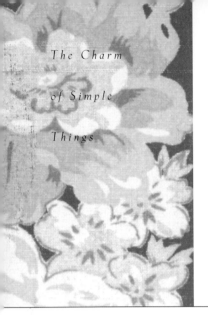

Come unto me all you who

labor and are heavy laden

and I will give you rest.

Matthew 11:28

Resting in God's Presence

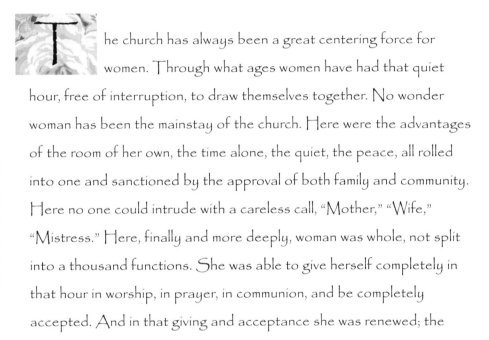

The church has always been a great centering force for women. Through what ages women have had that quiet hour, free of interruption, to draw themselves together. No wonder woman has been the mainstay of the church. Here were the advantages of the room of her own, the time alone, the quiet, the peace, all rolled into one and sanctioned by the approval of both family and community. Here no one could intrude with a careless call, "Mother," "Wife," "Mistress." Here, finally and more deeply, woman was whole, not split into a thousand functions. She was able to give herself completely in that hour in worship, in prayer, in communion, and be completely accepted. And in that giving and acceptance she was renewed; the springs were refilled.

Anne Morrow Lindbergh
Gift from the Sea

God worked very hard for six days and then stopped his labor to relax and luxuriate in what he had done. . . . It's hard to rest when there's so much to be done, but God wanted his people to know that resting is one of the most important things human beings can do.

David Roper

The Sabbath is more than an obligation, more than candles, wine, and religious services. It needs to be reframed so it can be what it was intended to be: A 24-hour protest against materialism, careerism, and competition. . . . The Sabbath is the ultimate statement that the world does not own us.

Jeffrey K. Salkin

The spiritual life and the love of God are knit right into the texture of our lives.

Leslie Williams

Sunday Go to Meetin'

The shiny black buggy . . . with a fringe on top, was the one in which Grandpa drove us to church. He allowed me to stand between his knees and hold the reins, even though I could not see over the horse's too-busy tail where we were going. But standing up on the back seat, I could see, squinting through the peephole window at the back, where the narrow wheels on a rainy Sunday sliced the road to chocolate ribbons. I got to hear Grandpa's voice on Sunday more than in all the rest of the week, because he sang in the choir; indeed, Grandpa led the choir.

Eudora Welty
One Writer's Beginnings

Solitude is a simple thing...

Solitude is a beautiful word. It sounds like sunlight through trees, or a walk on the beach, or a soprano voice that soars. . . . It's a different word than "alone"; I hear a moan in alone, which turns so easily into "loneliness," and has more to do with a single tree on a prairie or a child by herself on a crowded playground. Solitude is for those with an ample interior, with room to roam, well-provided with supplies. And I need a day or two, every so often, to make the journey.

Catherine Calvert
Victoria, September 1997

God is the friend of silence. We need to find God, but we cannot find Him in noise, in excitement.
Mother Teresa

Waiting in stillness, we

hear the absence of sound

become the presence of the

voice of God.

David Rensberger

A Garden Chair

Whenever I fall prey to the stress that adult life sends my way, I head to a place in my backyard, a place where a special chair sits near my garden. Among the birds singing their sweet songs and the butterflies amusing the rosemary and thyme, my childhood chair remains, inhaling the beauty that surrounds it.

My chair is the bridge to my past—an extension to days of innocence when life was simple and the hug of my father was enough. As my mother sat near me in her chair reading a magazine, the strenght of motherhood was instilled in me for life.

Yvette Pompa

A Little Corner of Heaven

Find a place to retreat, . . . a refuge where you can rest and be renewed before returning to the fray. Your corner of peace may be as simple as a comfortable chair with an old-fashioned lamp beside it. You turn on the lamp and sink into the chair in the circle of warm light. Or your peaceful place can be a book; you turn the page and step through the word windows into another world. . . .

Your place of retreat, your little corner of peace, may be very different from mine. The specifics don't really matter. The point is you find a place or an activity that gives your senses a chance to unwind and lets you catch a fresh vision of peacetime possibilities. Furnish it comfortably. Make it beautiful. Use it often.

Thomas Kinkaid
Simpler Times

Solitude has nurturing

qualities all its own.

Charles Swindoll

Patience is the continuous process of uncluttering what is around you and inside you.

Ingrid Trobisch

We live in a noisy, busy world. Silence and solitude are not twentieth-century words. They fit the era of Victorian lace, high-button shoes, and kerosene lamps better than our age of television, video arcades, and joggers wired with earphones. We have become a people with an aversion to quiet and an uneasiness with being alone.

Jean Fleming

The real problem of the Christian life comes where people do not usually look for it. It comes the very moment you wake up each morning. All your wishes and hopes for the day rush at you like wild animals. And the first job each morning consists simply in shoving them all back; in listening to that other voice, taking that other point of view, letting that other larger, stronger, quieter life come flowing in. And so on, all day. Standing back from all your natural fussings and frettings; coming in out of the wind.

C. S. Lewis
Mere Christianity

A journal is a simple thing...

In moments of solitude use a journal to record thoughts and insights, or quotes and verses that you want to remember. These journal entries can serve as signposts of meaningful stopovers along the path of life.

What to record in a journal:

1. names of books read and insights gained from them

2. inspirational thoughts gleaned from a time of solitude

3. favorite quotes from literature or real life

4. Bible verses to memorize

5. questions about life that puzzle you

6. a list of prayer petitions and answers

7. words of praise to God

A very strange
and solemn
feeling came over
me as I stood
there, with no
sound but the
rustle of the
pines, no one
near me,
and the sun
so glorious,
as for me
alone. It
seemed as
if I felt
God as I
never did
before, and I
prayed in my
heart that I might
keep that happy
sense of nearness all
my life.

**Louis May
Alcott**
(12 years old)

Prayer is a simple thing...

he saints of medieval days saw in everything a summons to prayer: the tolling of a bell, the flight of a swallow, the fall of a leaf. For myself, the best reminders are the people I meet:

The harried young woman who waits on me in a restaurant

The blasé secretary who greets me in an office

The weary old man who lies next door

All are reminders of the deep needs that lie all around me and that I cannot meet. All are incentives to prayer. I can do nothing for these men and women, but God can. I can pray for them silently as I encounter them, and ask God to use me or another instrument to make visible the invisible Christ.

David Roper
Elijah: A Man Like Us

The best prayer is to rest in the goodness of God, knowing that that goodness can reach right down to our lowest depths of need.

Julian of Norwich (b. 1342)

Moments on Her Knees

Mother Schaefer has a yardful of leaf-shedding trees, and she picks up every leaf unaided in spite of her sons' repeated protests. . . . "They just don't understand." [She explains.] "My basket and I want to do the job."

"You see, this life's just too busy nowadays. Everybody's busy rushing someplace so they can get back in time to rush someplace else. They want me to join this and that; they want me to go here and go there. It's all very nice, but they don't give me any time to think. I need to sort things out, to think them over and then talk about them—with God."

Even as she explained, the fragile little lady knelt and kept on with the work she loved so well. . . . She rubbed each leaf against her pale cheek as if to feel each tiny vein. . . . Then for a moment she closed her eyes, and I knew it was in prayer.

June Masters Bacher
Quiet Moments for Women

Thankfulness is a simple thing...

If you live thankfully you will live happily. You know how it is if you have a friend who moans all the time. It gets you down. It's boring. But if you live thankfully, that is, aware that everything, absolutely everything has been given by God, you will discover a treasure which will be with you for the rest of your life.

Christopher Herbert
A Little Prayer Diary

Simple things to be thankful for:

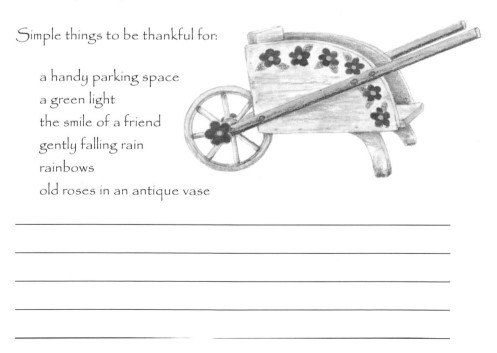

    a handy parking space
    a green light
    the smile of a friend
    gently falling rain
    rainbows
    old roses in an antique vase

_____

_____

_____

_____

_____

Joyful Thanks

_____

Spend one hour a day in

adoration of the Lord and

you'll be all right.

Mother Teresa
_____

raise is simply appreciation made public. When we enjoy an experience fully, we burst into happy, spontaneous praise. And we invite others to join in that praise: "Wasn't that a great meal?" "Isn't she beautiful?" "Isn't this a surprisingly good book?" We urge others to add their instruments to our grand symphony of delight, to play and sing and laugh with us, because we believe in its delightfulness. Even our hymns of joy invite heaven and earth to sing and for that sounding joy to be repeated.

Terry Lindvall
Surprised by Laughter

Wonderful Words of Life

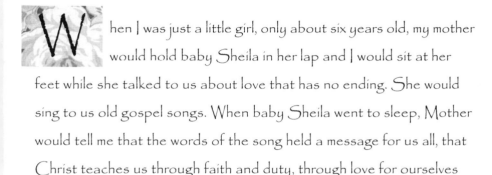

When I was just a little girl, only about six years old, my mother would hold baby Sheila in her lap and I would sit at her feet while she talked to us about love that has no ending. She would sing to us old gospel songs. When baby Sheila went to sleep, Mother would tell me that the words of the song held a message for us all, that Christ teaches us through faith and duty, through love for ourselves and others, how to live a rich and fulfilling life.

Sing them over again to me, wonderful words of life;
Let me more of their beauty see, wonderful words of life.

Jane Watson Hopping
The Pioneer Lady's Hearty Winter Cookbook

Were the whole realm of nature mine
That were an offering far too small.
Love so amazing, so divine
Demands my soul, my life, my all.

Isaac Watts
(1674–1748)

God in the Ordinary

If God only made his presence known in the momentous, how barren our lives would be of grace-filled windows to the sacred.

Instead, there are snowfalls and rain showers, waking and sleeping, as we live a succession of ordinary days. Into our ordinary world we are given this hidden God, one who comes to us as a baby born amid hay and barnyard smells to a nondescript couple on an ordinary night. Into the ordinary, came the extraordinary. The birth of a Savior. And our lives will never be the same.

Debra Klingsporn
Soul Searching

Acknowledgments

Grateful acknowledgment is made to the following publishers and copyright holders for permission to reprint copyrighted material.

June Masters Bacher, *Quiet Moments for Women* (Eugene, Or.: Harvest House, 1979). © Harvest House Publishers. Used by permission.

Emilie Barnes, *Secrets of the Garden* (Eugene, Or.: Harvest House Publishers, 1997). © Harvest House Publishers. Used by permission.

Ruth Haley Barton, "In a Material World," *Today's Christian Woman,* May/June, 1997, 465 Gunderson Dr., Carol Stream, IL. 60188.

Suzanne Bernes. *Victoria,* May 1996.

Michel Biehn, *Recipes from a Provençal Kitchen* (Reed Consumer Books, 1995).

Catherine Calvert, *Victoria,* December 1997.

Mary Mason Campbell, *The New England Butt'ry Shelf Cookbook* (Battleboro, Ver.: The Stephen Green Press, 1968).

Helen Colijn, *Song of Survivial: Women Interned* (Ashland, Or.: White Cloud Press,1995).

Harriet Crosby, *A Place Called Home* (Nashville: Thomas Nelson, 1997).

M. F. K. Fisher, *With Bold Knife and Fork* (New York: Konecky & Konecky, 1969).

Gloria Gaither, *We Have This Moment* (Nasvhille: Word, 1986). © Gloria Gaither.

Marjorie Holmes, *Lord Let Me Love* (New York: Bantam Doubleday Dell, 1978). © Marjorie Holmes.

Jane Watson Hopping, *The Lazy Days of Summer Cookbook* (New York: Villard Books, a division of Random House, 1992).

Jane Watson Hopping, *The Pioneer Lady's Hearty Winter Cookbook* (New York: Villard Books, a division of Random House, 1996).

Madeleine Kamman, *When French Women Cook* (New York: MacMillan Company, 1976).

W. Phillip Keller, *Taming Tension* (Grand Rapids: Baker Book House, 1979). © Phillip Keller.

Thomas Kinkaid, *Simpler Times* (Eugene, Or.: Harvest House Publishers, 1997). © 1997 by Harvest House Publishers, Eugene, Oregon. Used by permission.

Debra Klingsporn, *Soul Searching* (Nashville: Thomas Nelson, 1996).

Frank Levering and Wanda Urbanska, *Simple Living* (New York: Viking Penguin, 1992). © Frank Levering and Wanda Urbanska.

C. S. Lewis, *Mere Christianity* (London, HarperCollins, 1952).

Anne Morrow Lindbergh, *Gift from the Sea* (New York: Pantheon Books, a division of Random House, 1955). © 1955, 1975 by Anne Morrow Lindbergh.

Terry Lindvall, *Surprised by Laughter* (Nashville: Thomas Nelson, 1996).

Laura C. Martin, *Handmade Gifts from a Country Garden* (New York: Abbeville Press art books, 1994) © Laura C. Martin.

Belva Atkinson Murphy, *Mommie of the Mixing Bowl* (Chicago: Moody Press, 1959).

Kathleen Norris, *The Cloister Walk* (New York: Riverhead Books, a divison of G. P. Putnam's Sons, 1996). ©1996 Kathleen Norris.

Stacy and Paula Rinehart, *Living in Light of Eternity* (Colorado Springs: NavPress, 1986). © Stacy and Paula Rinehart.

David Roper, *A Man to Match the Mountain* (Grand Rapids, Mi.: Discovery House, 1998). Used by permission of Discovery House Publisher, Box 3566, Grand Rapids, MI. 49501. All rights reserved.

David Roper, *Elijah: A Man Like Us* (Grand Rapids, Mi.: Discovery House, 1996). Used by permission of Discovery House Publisher, Box 3566, Grand Rapids, MI. 49501. All rights reserved.

Edith Schaeffer, *The Tapestry* (Nashville: Word Inc., 1981).

Edith Schaeffer, *Common Sense Christian Living* (Nashville: Thomas Nelson, 1983.)

Charlie Shedd, *How to Make People Really Feel Loved* , © 1996 by Charlie W. Shedd. Published by Servant Publications, Box 8617, Ann Arbor, Michigan, 48107. Used with permission.

Elizabeth Skoglund, *A Quiet Courage* (Grand Rapids, Mi.: Baker Book House, 1997).

Alexandra Stoddard, *Living a Beautiful Life* (New York: Avon Books, a division of The Hearst Corporation, 1986). ©1986 Alexandra Stoddard.

Ingrid Trobisch, *Keeper of the Springs* (Sisters, Or.: Multnomah Gift Books, a division of Multonomah Publishers, Inc., 1997). © Ingrid Trubisch, 1997.

Eudora Welty, *One Writer's Beginnings* (Cambridge, Mass: Harvard University Press, 1984).

Laura Ingalls Wilder, *Words from a Fearless Heart* (Nashville: Broadman & Holman, 1996).

Laura Ingalls Wilder, *Saving Graces* (Nashville: Broadman & Holman, 1997).

Leslie Williams, *Night Wrestling* (Nashville: Word, Inc., 1996).

Alan D. Wright, *A Chance at Childhood Again* (Sisters, Or.: Multnomah Publishers, 1997). © by Alan D. Wright, 1997.